THE RAINMAKER SOLUTION

by Joel Johnson

Copyright © Joel Johnson

All rights reserved.

ISBN-13: 978-0615795256

ISBN-10: 0615795250

CreateSpace, North Charleston, SC

Big Man Publishing

Note:

Joel Johnson is a Certified Financial Planner® and an investment advisor representative. As such, some of the topics discussed in this material are appropriate for use by dually licensed producers only. Discussion of securities and securities transactions by those lacking the appropriate registration places their insurance license at risk.

Results from the use of these concepts may not be representative of the experience of all financial professionals and is no guarantee of future success. Your results may vary.

THE RAINMAKER SOLUTION

by Joel Johnson

Welcome to the Rainmaker Solution. In creating this strategy, I wanted to produce a step-by-step plan to help reduce the stress and pressure in the lives of producers by creating a financial services practice model that multiplies results through multiple sales channels. What I discovered – which many of you can likely relate to – is that as my business grew and we crossed that $1.5 million in revenues mark as a firm, I was feeling increasingly stressed. Yes, much more successful. But much more stressed.

To the outside world, it looked like, "Wow, I'm doing great. I'm getting all these awards, I'm up on stages presenting, and everything's fantastic." Inside, I was tired; I wished I could take more time off without the business stopping. I reached a ceiling of complexity where I was constrained by my time and all kinds of tasks that had nothing to do with marketing or selling. That was the impetus for designing the Rainmaker Solution.

The Rainmaker Solution is simply a way in which I could build a practice that was not completely dependent on *me* to do the selling.

Years ago, you and I got into this business to have freedom – to have freedom of time, freedom of income and to be able to do things that very few of our friends could do. At some point along the way, I'd begun to feel like a slave to my business. That is the purpose of writing the guide you have in front of you – to create more freedom in your life by leveraging this

Rainmaker Solution.

If I could create the traffic – meaning the flow of appointments – and have well-trained salespeople to process those appointments, I thought I could create a lot of freedom for myself. That's what I wanted to do, and this guide is simply the step-by-step plan I followed to reduce stress and pressure and create a life for myself that has a lot more financial freedom than many of us may have ever dreamed possible.

The potential benefits of this strategy are a more predictable cash flow and a much higher quality of life, including more time with the people you love and doing the things you care about.

A QUICK WORD OF WARNING: This Rainmaker Solution is not for everyone. Some people just want to exist as a single-office producer. For the solo producer, I have a solo Rainmaker Solution where you can apply many of these principles to a single producer office.

However, if you buy into this philosophy of the Rainmaker multiple producer office, then your profits and cash flow can be greatly multiplied while your freedom is increased. You will shift from being a salesman to truly being a business owner, and the possible growth for your business is limitless.

"Special Note" – You will also own a saleable business where you build true equity and value to sell some day.

Take a quick look at where you stand today – whether that's half a million dollars in revenues to your financial services practice or $2 to $3 million. Envision tripling that revenue while at the same time increasing the quality of your life. Imagine increasing your bottom line while eliminating frustration and multiplying your confidence because you can be out for a day, a week or even a month and still your business runs smoothly.

The alternative? You could continue to live in the rut in which, from an outsider's perspective, you look very successful while on the inside you're terribly discontented and frustrated – knowing there's something more out there, but feeling stuck. Let's face it. No one wants that feeling. You know in your gut there's so much more yet you are stifled! The Rainmaker Solution is the ability to truly "break through" to build a financial services practice that allows you to do only what you're great at, removing all the things that drain your energy, surrounding yourself with people who can help you make a great living and keeping your practice going whether *you* are there or not.

CHAPTER 1 — PROTECTING CONFIDENCE AND ENERGY

A few years back, I came into the office, and I remember being very excited to be there. I had a nice, full day of appointments planned, and my focus was laser sharp driving in. I had three prospects lined up whom I'd never met before. They were leads from my radio program and already expressed an interest in getting a second opinion. Those are always good leads because they are screened ahead of time, so I know I'm walking into quality appointments. Then, I also had three closing appointments scheduled – second or third appointments – in which we were likely to move the ball forward. (In our first appointments, I identify whom we may be able to help, decide whom I want to work with, and they decide if they think we're a good fit. If we can come to an agreement and a comfort level on the implementation, we're ready for the follow-up appointment, which we call "a close.")

So, there I was – heading into the perfect day with six appointments. Three pre-qualified opening appointments and three solid closing appointments in which I would likely close business. And what happened? I hit the office doors, and immediately my staff began asking me questions like, "Mr. Jones needs his required minimum distribution, so what should we liquidate from his account to satisfy that?" Someone else immediately started hitting me with, "The lease is running out on our satellite office out east. If we want to renew it, you're going to need to look over this lease this morning." Then my operations manager wanted to talk to me about summer marketing events, and *immediately* my energy level was drained right out of me. Stuff, stuff, stuff... am I passionate about any of it?

No! Is it important? Yes. Do I have to handle it? No!

This kind of morning is one of the most common occurrences you must protect against if you're going to embrace the Rainmaker Solution. You've got to protect your confidence. You've got to protect your energy. You've got to protect your focus. In fact, if you have any employees, their #1 job is to protect your confidence and energy... period. You are a performer, an athlete if you will. Frank Sinatra didn't tune pianos, and Peyton Manning doesn't make his own travel arrangements. They focus on what the world pays them for.

I know I can be much more productive if I focus on two or three things, at the most, as a producer. Some days, I may literally need to focus on just one, but certainly no more than two or three things. For me, those focuses are how I am going to drive traffic into my business, the messaging required to do that and how to effectively address the needs of the prospects who walk through my doors.

Personally, I love to be a strategic thinker who *starts* things. I submit to you that if you're a producer who really wants to *own* your business, your job is to start things – not finish them. I love to come into the office and start things, and I would simply suggest to you that you cannot be *starting* things if you constantly have your staff pulling you into the past. Be present- and future-based and guard against past-based thinking.

I think most of us would agree Bill Gates is one of the greatest entrepreneurs of our time. Interestingly enough, he simplified something that was very complex and subsequently made billions of dollars. Some of you have the gift of simplifying things for your clients. This is why they buy from you. I think one of the things that had to just drain the energy out of Bill Gates was his involvement in the anti-trust case brought against Microsoft. He was continually required to go back and review conversations and e-mails that took place years prior, answering questions from attorneys about what he meant when he sent various communications. I can only imagine the drudgery this type of "past tense" thinking cause for such an innovative and forward-thinking individual. If you're reading this guide, I would venture to guess you might share some of Bill Gates' characteristics. I'd bet there's a good chance you *thrive* on moving things forward. When you get sucked into the past, it feels as if your passion and energy are literally being drained. If so, you and I share that in common.

These days, my ideal focus day involves no "past tense" thinking. Instead, it simply entails coming in with laser sharp focus, creating new appointments and seeing people. I'm seeing fewer and fewer people in my practice at this point because I've trained my team so *they* can meet with prospects as long as I "make the rain." I feed the prospect funnel, and we are succeeding because my time and effort is focused on the future and the present – not the past.

Again, the purpose of this book is to give you a step-by-step process of creating the Rainmaker Solution. However, in order to do that, there are certain criteria that must be met. There are certain "buy-ins," to use the corporate vernacular, that must be met in your mind if you are to move successfully forward. If you're unable to meet some of these criteria, I would simply question whether you're really just a salesperson or whether you genuinely want to create a business that you legitimately own. Remember, a salesperson has to show up every day to sell to make a commission. A business owner builds a structure that is not completely dependent on him.

Sometimes a business owner obviously needs to be present to create momentum or set things in motion in the business, but he or she is not required to tend to the minutia. For instance, take a look at Oprah. Oprah's many business ventures do depend on her as the brand and the face person, but there are thousands of things that go on behind the scenes in her operations that she has absolutely no part in. Consider other similar "celebrity brands" that have achieved significant levels of success, and they will generally have this in common. The leaders communicate a vision or solution to get things started.

In the Rainmaker Solution, you want to be "the face" of your organization but not the one responsible for execution of trivial details. When you've achieved this shift, a beautiful thing occurs. When you take a week's vacation, when you step out of the business, heck – if you leave this world forever – the business continues on.

CHAPTER 2 – EIGHT CRITERIA YOU MUST AGREE WITH

Let's dive into the specific criteria that must be met in order for you to go onto the next step of this book. *First, you must have structures and systems in place.* That doesn't mean you need to be the one continually designing them, but they must be in place. For instance, in my practice we have a system in place to set appointments. The system is based upon specific criteria when prospects call in, and there is a decision using that criteria as to <u>who</u> in my firm will see that particular prospect. If a prospect meets a certain standard, they are scheduled to sit down with me. I want them to have at least $600,000 of investable assets – preferably a million dollars and above – but the bottom line is that there is a structure in place so that I personally *never* decide who to see. My staff makes that decision.

In my firm, I know if someone ends up on my calendar there's a good reason for it. If they don't meet my set criteria, I try not to question my staff, and this is a critical point. My staff is very well-trained at what they do. If, for some reason, a prospect sees me and they don't meet a certain financial criteria, I know without any question that my staff must have believed it was important for me to see that person, and I trust in them and the processes we have in place.

Another example of a structure that is in place in our firm is our bookkeeping procedure. I don't pay attention to every bill being paid. I approve big systems. We recently had to do a significant technology upgrade. My office manager had all the research done by outside people and then gave a proposal to me. I had those recommendations reviewed by my staff. I asked three questions of my staff. "Do we need to do this? Is this the best thing we can do? Should we actually be doing *more* at this time so that we don't have to re-do this a year or two from now?" After hearing their answers to those simple questions, I gave them the nod to proceed. My time on this was about seven minutes. I have no exact idea when that system is going to be implemented. I trust in my team to work out those details. I've hired people whom I believe genuinely care about our company, and I rest in that belief. That leads to the second criteria that must be met.

For the Rainmaker Solution to succeed, *you've got to surround yourself with people you trust*. You must trust your people implicitly. It's imperative that you make your hiring decisions "with your gut" and with data. Sure, applicants at your firm should obviously meet certain proficiency standards, but go with your gut. Can you trust your people? I trust mine with my very livelihood. I know they're loyal to me, and I know they are part of a team that wouldn't make decisions based on self-interest or self-promotion – trying to get a leg up on another person within our organization. We simply don't have that culture in our company, and I think it's very, very important.

Now, that sounds a bit utopian, right? Everyone bought into the mission, trustworthy and focused on the same mission? How in the world do you build *that*? In my firm, I've done so by making myself a little vulnerable. I'm open with my team. I'm open with some of my fears – at least those that wouldn't destroy the confidence of my staff. For example, I share some of the concerns I have when we make various financial commitments without really knowing what the outcome is going to be. I literally sit down with them and say, "You know, I honestly don't know how this is going to turn out. This is a big financial commitment we're making this year, but I trust you to come to me if it's not working, and I trust that I don't need to know exactly how this is going to work because I believe in *you* and your ability to make it work." Simple as it may sound, I believe in my team, and if you put structures in place and genuinely trust your people, it will give you a tremendous amount of freedom. By the way, some of you should be embarrassed at how little you pay your employees. If you're good at what you do, you're in a 40% federal bracket. That means it only costs you $6,000 to pay someone an extra $10,000. Think about the difference it makes in someone's life if they go from $40,000 of income to $50,000 of income. It is a huge difference for them and their family. Pay your people well.

Let me stop here and say this: some of you simply *cannot* make this leap of trusting. It's important to pause and address this because this one thing could be the biggest factor holding you back from the success and freedom you *could* be enjoying. Often because of your background, many of you have a hard time trusting others. Every transaction you enter into – let's say it's with a field marketing organization or a new broker dealer – you head into with a mindset of trying to protect yourself. You go into that situation trying to make sure that you're not being taken advantage of. Spoiler alert: you're *going* to be taken advantage of in life. And the more you try to protect yourself against that reality, the more you're going to weigh yourself down and hold yourself back. In my opinion, it's much more enjoyable to go forward in life trying to serve others – trying to create real value for those in your marketplace. You're not going to win every deal. You'll get into agreements that possibly weren't the best in the world, but life will go on. Personally, I think we'll get to the end of this lifetime and look at our loved ones, our employees, our employee's children and maybe even their grandchildren that we've impacted, and *that* is going to be our satisfaction.

When it's all said and done, if my field marketing organization made a few extra basis points and maybe I could've cut a better deal, or if my broker dealer could've given me a little higher payout and they didn't, *who cares?* When I get to the end of my life, how much money can I really spend? So instead, I tend to think life is about serving others. In order to serve others, you've got to start by trusting others – even in the face of the knowledge that from time to time, you're going to get burnt.

If trusting others is a lifelong struggle for you, I would encourage you to dig down deep, possibly even get some outside help and work to uncover the roots of that pattern in your life that makes you constantly try to protect yourself. You might get your hands on some resources from people like Tony Robbins, Dan Sullivan or some of the other great business coaches out there because if you walk through life constantly worried that you're going to get taken advantage of, I *promise* you that you will not grow your business or your life to its full potential.

THE TIME SYSTEM

The next criteria to fully embrace in order for the Rainmaker Solution to work in your practice is *the concept of free time, buffer time and focus time in your life*. I will credit this to one of my personal coaches,

Dan Sullivan of Strategic Coach. He is one person who had a big impact on me in my business (and maybe even my emotional and spiritual peace of mind). Dan preaches that you've got to create free time, buffer time and focus time. Take time off to think. Shut off the iPhone. Turn off the e-mail. Look out the window. Take a walk. Leave the radio off when you're driving into the office. Allow your mind to breathe because if you can master this task, you will have a leg up on the vast majority of the competition. Most people don't know how to structure their time – they don't know how to take free time. When they're with their family, they're thinking about work. When they're at work, they're regretting the fact that they didn't take time to go to their kid's dance recital or Little League game.

In this information era, we seem to have lost the

ability to take free time. Create it. Block it out on your calendar. Then there's buffer time. I was describing buffer time earlier in this book when I was talking about the day I was driving into the office. I had those three great first appointments and three great second appointments, and then I got interrupted with all that other stuff. All that other stuff is buffer activity – it's administrative activity. It's important, and maybe I need to address it – maybe I don't – but it does not need to be addressed on a focus day. My focus days should be centered only on the things I am good at and in which I move the ball down the field – focus days are offensive time. Administrative tasks are buffer time, and for me, those fall on Fridays and the first four hours on Monday. Monday morning, we have our staff meetings and my key team leader meetings.

Then I'm off and running for the week, so Monday

afternoon, Tuesday, Wednesday and Thursday are my core focus days, and then Friday wraps up my week as a buffer day. I've structured my life that way because it makes my staff a lot happier. They know there are going to be certain times they can come to me and interrupt me, and they also know there are certain times when I'm simply not to be disturbed. I'm focused in the zone, Intense! You've got to create free time, buffer time and focus time.

Another criterion in order to implement all these strategies and have success is to *identify what you truly sell*. Stop for just a second and think about that simple question: What do you really sell? Do you *really* think that when people come into your office and you get paid a $10,000 or $20,000 commission to sell an annuity, a mutual fund, a securities transaction or bring in a big fee-based account, do you really think the client bought that *product*? Do you really think your strategy is so unique in the marketplace that the *strategy* is what they bought?

Nonsense. They didn't just buy a product or a strategy. In fact, let's take ABC annuity for instance. Clients can buy ABC annuity from at least 1,000 other people (and maybe 200,000 other people). They're not only buying the product you're selling – they're buying *you*. They're buying something you said. They're buying the way you and your team made them *feel*. So understand what you sell. It's not just about the product. Many of you are working with outside vendors, broker dealers, field marketing organizations, mutual fund companies and money management firms who have you convinced that they've got a little bit of an extra edge – that somehow they know how to manage money better than someone else, their annuity is better and if you can just communicate that edge to the client, they'll buy it. Let me assure you, if you sell a product, you will be commoditized in a heartbeat because someone will come along and offer it for cheaper. You've got to figure out what you really sell.

It is you!

In our firm, I'll tell you exactly what we sell. In fact, here is our branding statement:

By using the best tools and strategies available, my team and I take the <u>fear</u> out of your financial future and give you <u>confidence</u> in what lies ahead.

In your personal business, you need to remove your personal fear and build your confidence, and that's what we try to do for our clients, as well. I can't emphasize this point enough – understand what you sell. As long as you think you sell a product, just pause and think about Wal-Mart for a moment. You'll eventually be shut down by someone who's much bigger with a lot more money to throw around.

The next criterion for fully implementing the Rainmaker Solution is your *willingness to bring in salespeople.* If you're creating a practice in which you are the Rainmaker, you've got to have salespeople who can close deals. Now, I use the word salespeople very loosely here, and let me tell you why. We test our people. We use a test called the Prevue Assessment on all our team members. We also use a Kolbe test, which tests for people's instinctual talents – the ways they inherently work best. We've used a number of different tests out there. The theory is you work on your strengths, not your weaknesses. If all you do in life is work on your weaknesses, you're likely to just have mediocre weaknesses, and that isn't going to get you ahead. If you ignore your weaknesses and work on your strengths, now you're thinking like Michael Jordan, Frank Sinatra or Michael Jackson. Michael Jackson was probably a *horrible* businessman, and you know what? It didn't matter. He was so good at the two or three things he did well that money just flowed to him, and there was a lot of room for sloppiness in other areas of life. Stop trying to be good at too many things and step into a world of freedom and excitement.

Our salespeople often don't "test" like great salespeople – they really don't. I was shocked when we did Kolbe tests on them. I work with some outside consultants, and I started asking them how our salespeople could score the way they do and close so much business. I said, "Why are we so productive when we measure ourselves with other organizations and my salespeople don't test like great salespeople?" The answer that came back surprised me. I was told, "Joel, when prospects come into your office, they're confident about working with your firm because of the communication they've had with you – because of the setup that you've done whether it's through the radio program or your seminars, etc. People are coming in ready to hear how you may be able to help them, and when your salespeople reinforce your message it can make it that much easier to implement what may already be going on in the minds of the potential customer."

Whether my model of "pre-conditioning" prospects is your model or whether you really do need skilled salespeople to handle the process from the start, I'll leave that for you to determine, but either way, you've got to bring in outside salespeople. If you think *you* have to see all the appointments, I've got bad news for you. There are only 168 hours in a week, and I would suggest that your greatest limitation may be how you split your time.

In my firm, I'm not limited by my own time. I have three other salespeople, and I'm currently in the process of hiring another. A good friend of mine with a practice in Florida has 10 plus salespeople. If you position your practice properly in this Rainmaker Solution model, you are only limited by your ability to communicate suitable strategies to your clients, so hire enough people to process that traffic.

Another criterion requires you *eliminate distractions and people who take away your energy*. I talked earlier about those buffer days – those administrative tasks that I think you need to reduce in order to be a good Rainmaker. Again, my friend Dan Sullivan doesn't even use e-mail. He doesn't have an office. He is the perfect model of eliminating distractions in his life. He only does what he does best, which is creating content to inspire and guide other entrepreneurs. If you ask him what the net profit was on his organization last month, my guess would be he probably has no idea. He's not concerned. He doesn't care because he's got people in place that will take care of that piece for him. By the way, his organization did over $25 million in revenues last year and he started as a one-on-one coach. See the correlation – one-on-one coaching to leader and Rainmaker; one-on-one financial sales to leader and Rainmaker.

Removing the people who take away your energy can be difficult, and it's difficult because as an entrepreneur, I want to add value to people's lives. It's hard for me to let somebody go. It's even hard to not hire somebody I feel needs a little help or maybe just needs a break. I have to be very cautious of that. I also need to be cautious about keeping people on my team who zap my energy. If you're not already sure who those people are in your office, here's a quick test. When you walk into the office each morning, who's the first person you *look forward* to seeing? Who's the person you'd rather not see before you start your day?

If you avoid someone in your office , that might be a great indicator of a problem. Maybe that person shouldn't be in your organization. I'm not telling you to walk right in tomorrow and hand out pink slips, but be aware that certain people increase our confidence and energy level. Others drain our confidence and zap the energy out of us, and we can't wait to end conversations with them and move on. I would submit that if those people are in your organization, you either need to avoid contact with them or consider helping them move to a position or an organization that's better suited for them. Believe me, they're not benefiting if they're not a good fit in your organization,.

The next criteria necessary for making the most of this Rainmaker Solution is truly *deciding what you want.* One of the people I have tremendously benefited from knowing over the last few years is Mike Meek. He's a strategic business consultant, and he came in and completely reorganized our management structure when I bought out a former partner a little while ago. The first thing Mike told me was, "You've got to figure out what you want because we can't do anything great until you know that." Now, that obviously sounds really easy because we can say well, we want a lot of money, we want financial security, etc. Those are the quick, shallow answers. But take a day, take a blank piece of paper (not a computer keyboard where you'll be tempted to check your e-mail) and start to write out what you want in more specific terms. Then you can build your organization around serving that purpose, and believe me, your people will get behind someone who knows what they want.

The last criterion to implement the Rainmaker Solution is to *recognize the risk of where you currently stand*. What do I mean by that? Are you an entrepreneur who has a sales job, or are you a true entrepreneur who can focus on your unique abilities? If you have to do all the selling, there is a lot of risk in your life. You see, I contend that there are three different types of entrepreneurs. I think the vast majority of people who say they're entrepreneurs are really just salespeople. Yes, they're self-employed. Yes, when they sell, they make money. Maybe they have an assistant or two, and maybe they even have an organization of eight to 10 people, but they're *completely* dependent upon their own ability to go out and sell. I'd submit that this description applies to a very high percentage of "entrepreneurs." I'm certainly not saying that's a bad way to live. You can make any amount of money you want by selling, but quite frankly, I want to take time off when I want to take time off. I want to be with my kids. I want to be with my wife. I want to travel, and I don't want my business to take a break any time I get the urge to do so. Therefore, I don't want to be that kind of entrepreneur (the "pure salesperson").

I think the second type of entrepreneur is one who

could be described as a "lifestyle" entrepreneur. This type of individual may also be a salesperson or a business owner; they're not necessarily driven as much by money but by lifestyle. When they get to a certain level or annual revenue, they just stop working. I have a good friend who fits this mold perfectly. If he has a big January and makes a bunch of money, he will be hunting in February. He'll be catching all the NASCAR races down south. He'll have a great time until that bank account starts to go down again, and then he'll head back to work. There's absolutely nothing wrong with this approach either, but is that the type of entrepreneur you really are? Or are you the entrepreneur who I contend is maybe only one percent of all entrepreneurs – the individual driven by growth? For this type of person, it's not about money. It's not about lifestyle. It's about competing against yourself more than anyone else.

You're always a little restless and discontent. You live for the "game." That's me. I am constantly wondering if I'm good enough to take this business of mine to the next level, and for entrepreneurs like us, it is all about growth.

I drive my wife, Wendy, a little crazy from time to time. She'll ask me, "Joel, why can't you just be happy with where you're at? You've done pretty well!" But, for me, it's not about "doing well." It's about whether or not I can grow. Some may see that as being discontent or greedy. I assure you, that's not what it's about. Those of you that understand what I'm saying right now know that it's not all about money, although money is nice. Those who are wired like us are happier when they're growing. Sure, we want to look back and feel a sense of accomplishment, but we also want to look forward and wonder if we could top ourselves. Much like a basketball player – could I jump that high or score that many or compete against that person? Am I really in this league? For me, that's what it's about.

Thus, recognizing which type of entrepreneur you are is critical. Are you an entrepreneur with a sales job, or are you an entrepreneur who wonders if you can compete on a much higher level?

THE RAINMAKER SOLUTION – STRATEGIES CONTENT PART 2

12 OBSTACLES AND STRATEGIES TO A RAINMAKER BUSINESS MODEL

Obstacle 1 – "I don't know what I want."
Strategy – Use the three-year question.

Obstacle 2 – "I don't see how this can work."
Strategy – If you don't believe, borrow someone else's belief and confidence.

Obstacle 3 – "People want to see me."
Strategy – Communicate that you are leading the team and directing their investment and insurance choices. You are in charge.

Obstacle 4 – "I'm not organized and structured for this."

Strategy – Write out what your firm would look like if you never did a first appointment.

Obstacle 5 – "I'm bogged down and frustrated with non-revenue generating activities."

Strategy – Make a list. / Clear the list!

Obstacle 6 – "I don't have the right producers on my team."

Strategy – Build proper support staff first. Then focus your time on your top three activities.

Obstacle 7 – "Distractions take up all my energy."

Strategy – Use the energy litmus test. / Protect your confidence and energy.

Obstacle 8 – "I lack clarity in my sales process."

Strategy – Map out and systematize your process.

Obstacle 9 – "My team won't go along."

Strategy – Get them involved early, communicate your vision and explain how they will benefit.

Obstacle 10 – "I can't possibly manage all of this. I can't control it."

Strategy – Build working leaders but <u>NOT</u> layers of management.

Obstacle 11 – "Will incremental growth be worth it?"

Strategy - Set huge goals to transform your business.

Obstacle 12 - "I can't afford this." or "I need to personally keep my sales up for the cash flow."
Strategy - Make decisions and dream as if money is no longer an issue.

In the first part of this book, I told you a lot about my philosophy and about some of the things that, frankly, we have to agree upon in order for The Rainmaker Solution to work for you. I call them criteria for implementing the Rainmaker Solution. I've included a little strategy and a few specific steps, but for the most part, thus far, we've talked at a philosophical level.

Now, let's transition to the very specific strategies and things you need to adopt in order to make this Rainmaker Solution truly come to life. In this book, I'm primarily talking about a multiple producer practice — meaning a practice in which there is a "lead" producer and perhaps one or two associate producers working under him or her. Some of the general philosophies I share can also be taken and utilized in a single producer office, but for those specific tips and strategies, please reference my supporting book, *The Solo Rainmaker Solution*. This book will deal in much more detail with how to take a single producer office and become a Rainmaker even when you *do* handle all appointments yourself. The solo Rainmaker solution is tailored for a producer doing between $500,000 to $1 million of revenues – wanting to grow to $1.5 million or $1.75 million so his or her net income is between $750,000 and $1 million. (I think you can get to that level as a single producer. You may not be building a lot of saleable value in your business overall, but you can be living a tremendous life if you fit this bill.) If this accurately describes you, stay tuned for this sole producer resource. The book you have in your hand has been designed primarily to build the multi-producer practice.

So let's dive in. What we're doing here is laying out the simple steps to achieve a practice that is not dependent upon a single producer. Keep in mind the payoffs as we enter into this next section. As a producer successfully implementing The Rainmaker Solution:

- You can have a much more predictable cash flow.

- You can free up an incredible amount of personal time.

- You can create a tremendous amount of flexibility in your life.

- You can be present, and therefore, excited about the future instead of being constantly pulled into the past to deal with problems.

- You can focus your time on the creative side of your brain.

- You can be *people*-focused – not *problem*-

focused.

So how do you get *there* from where you currently stand? Let's take a look at both the obstacles you might face and the strategies you'll need to overcome them.

OBSTACLE 1 – "I DON'T KNOW WHAT I WANT."
STRATEGY – USE THE THREE-YEAR QUESTION.

Obstacle number one is not knowing what you want out of your practice. The solution or the strategy is to make a very specific determination about what you'd like your practice to look like in the years to come. Write this description down and get as detailed as you possibly can. For me, the "three-year question" works wonderfully. Perhaps you've used a similar question when meeting with your clients. Not familiar with "the three-year question"? Here it is: *If I were sitting here three years from today and I looked back over the last three years, what would have had to happen for me to be happy with my progress?* (I credit this question to Dan Sullivan)

This question absolutely forces you to think as if the future has already happened.

Let me read you something that I wrote to myself on April 1, 2012. (As I pen this book, I'm roughly a year down the line from making these little notes to myself.)

"It is April 1, 2015. My firm has grown to $6.6 million in revenues."

"I'm dominating the non-Fairfield County, Connecticut, market."

(For those of you that are not familiar with Connecticut, Connecticut's a state of about four million people and about a million of them live in a part of Connecticut called Fairfield County, which is really just a suburb of New York City. In our firm, we separate that market out. We want to dominate the *non*-Fairfield County, Connecticut, market.)

"I am the go-to media expert for all things related to financial planning – TV, radio, newspaper – you name it. I am the number one source for them when they have any questions regarding financial planning."

"I have three other producers who are just as effective at the one-on-one sales process as I am."

"I have a performance-based culture within my organization."

"I am a hero to my employees." (I don't mean 'hero' in a weird way, but I'm seen as someone they can count on – somebody they know cares for them.)

"I work four days a week and 44 weeks a year."

"I have flawless customer service."

I'll be honest with you, customer service was an area in which we struggled a little because of our incredibly fast growth. However, I determined that I wanted no client question to go unanswered for more than 24 hours, and I wanted my employees to have the knowledge base to handle all issues that could possibly arise.

"I have $150 million of assets under management in fee-based accounts."

We bill 1.5 percent on our assets, so if I can have $150 million in assets under management in fee-based accounts, that's roughly $2.1 million of net revenues after we pay for some outsourcing services we utilize.

"I have developed a high net worth clientele."

In our firm, we've built the practice on what I call "the middle-class millionaire." Most of our clients have between $500,000 and $2 million of investable assets. I wanted to carve out a niche in the high net worth area and have certain clientele with $5 million or more in investable assets – likely meaning they have between $2-$5 million with our firm.

"I have a partnership structure in which I control the firm, but high performers within my firm have equity in either the main company or one of the underlying entities."

There you have it – a pretty clear idea of what I was thinking at the time. Now, please understand that my goals shouldn't inherently be yours. Every producer's goals and vision are unique. But this should give you a clear idea of the thought process that went into determining "what I wanted." Decide what you want, and write it down as though you're already sitting there three years from now looking back. There is incredible power in visualizing the results you desire *before* they ever happen.

OBSTACLE 2 – "I DON'T SEE HOW THIS CAN WORK."
STRATEGY – IF YOU DON'T BELIEVE, BORROW SOMEONE ELSE'S BELIEF AND CONFIDENCE.

Obstacle number two is simply not being able to visualize how this Rainmaker Solution could ever really work. What you're struggling with here is a question of belief. For many producers (and people in general), your mind inherently sees all the obstacles first. It's not naturally inclined to see how a solution *could* work.

Therefore, you've got to anchor in on real-life examples. You've got to believe that someone else believes. If you can't believe how you can do it, find someone who has already done it – someone with bigger vision, someone with two or three times your production or success – and simply know that they believe. Piggyback on someone else's belief initially if you must, but you have *got* to find something to grasp onto at this point to believe deep in your soul that you can grow to the level you desire.

Okay, so strategy number one is determine what you want. Number two is even if you don't believe what you want can actually be achieved, pinpoint your vision and grab hold of someone whose vision and belief can serve as a guiding light.

OBSTACLE 3 – "PEOPLE WANT TO SEE ME."

STRATEGY – COMMUNICATE THAT YOU ARE LEADING THE TEAM AND DIRECTING THEIR INVESTMENT AND INSURANCE CHOICES. YOU ARE IN CHARGE.

Obstacle number three. This is a big one. "People only want to see *me*." The people coming to your seminars, the people referred to you, the people who may hear your radio program – you're often inclined to assume they only want to sit down with you. From personal experience, I don't think that's true. Some people do want to see you, but most rational individuals know that you are overseeing things, that you're the communicator, that you are in control and that you're generally supervising their investment strategies. That said, they don't necessarily need to always see *you*.

Now, I know you may be sitting there right this very

moment struggling with what I just said, so let me give you some real-life examples. If Suze Orman opened a mutual fund tomorrow called the Suze Orman Mutual Fund and somebody wanted to open an account, do you think they would realistically expect to meet with Suze? Do you really think they would ever anticipate sitting across a table from her? Of course not. That's ridiculous. So why would they buy her fund? I submit to you, whether you like Suze Orman or not (and I'll spare you my opinion), I will say she's effectively built a media empire. If she opened a Suze Orman Mutual Fund, I would expect it to raise $1 billion very, very quickly. Why? Because people trust the brand. They trust her. If a potential client had to come in to see someone else to open that account, it likely wouldn't matter a bit that they weren't meeting with Suze herself. This is how I'd encourage you to begin to envision and position your practice.

Think about it from a practice standpoint. Ric Edelman, a consummate Rainmaker in our industry, is the true brand of his firm. He's on the radio offering his philosophy, but he has associate financial advisors who meet with prospects all over the country that want to join Edelman Financial. Those prospects *never* sit down with Ric. He is living proof this model can and does work – people do not necessarily need to see you, and you *can* structure your firm in such a way that you don't have to remain the bottleneck – the limit – by seeing everyone who walks through the doors.

The clients you have outgrown want to talk to you. Ten years ago we would meet with somebody who had a $40,000 CD and that's all the money they had, and we promised them annual reviews every single year. Now I'm running a $4.5-$5 million a year company and I promised somebody who gave me $40,000 10 years ago annual reviews. This is a tough one. I think you've got to be honest with the clients here. I think they need to know that you are still running the firm, that you're still setting strategies and that you care deeply about them. And I think that you do need to offer them reviews if they want the reviews, but you do not personally do the reviews. Give them the annual reviews you promised, but this is a wonderful training ground for your new Associate Producer. A great way to bring on another producer is to train them to do these reviews. I brought on somebody a year ago and these reviews have generated additional sales to existing clients that I may not have been devoting a lot of time to. That's a fantastic situation for somebody who comes out of a captive or brokerage system where they're used to just pounding the phones for prospects. They can do your reviews, write potential additional business and learn to bring in some business on their own.

As I sit here and write this book, one of the things I'm dealing with is this very issue in my practice. What I have done that has been successful is I've communicated to the clients that if you really want to own competitive products to meet your needs and build confidence in what you're doing, I've got to have time to research those products and stay on top of those investment strategies. My team is very well trained to meet with you. I have Certified Financial Planners™ on my team. I have people with a lot of education on my team. I have to make sure you own the right stuff and I'm monitoring that behind the scenes.

Some people you just might need to let go, which is sad. They will find other firms. You can do this in a way to be nice to the clients and you still fulfill your promises to everyone, and if they choose to leave, then let them leave graciously. Appreciate them – thank them. Out of the 1,000 households that we serve, we probably lost three last year.

OBSTACLE 4 — "I'M NOT ORGANIZED AND STRUCTURED FOR THIS."

STRATEGY — WRITE OUT WHAT YOUR FIRM WOULD LOOK LIKE IF YOU NEVER DID A FIRST APPOINTMENT.

Obstacle number four is that your company is not organized to allow for these systems. The hard pill to swallow here is that it may be time to re-think your company. Take a blank piece of paper – maybe even set this book down right now to do this – and draw out what your practice would look like if you never held another appointment.

Yes, you're driving the firm's success. Yes, you're communicating the firm's message. If you market by seminars, you're still likely the one conducting them. If you market by referrals, you're communicating with your clients the importance of their referrals and introductions, and you can do this with a marketing piece and a DVD. But when a new prospect comes into your office, what if you just walked out and greeted them in the lobby, and the appointment was run by someone else? What if you only conducted second appointments – leaving the intake appointments to associates? It *can* be done. It *absolutely can* be done. So, if you haven't yet, take time to complete this radical exercise and draw out what your practice would look like if you never sat down for another appointment.

Now, I want to refer you to an important diagram here in the book. Let's look for a moment at the Single Producer Practice chart. In a single producer practice, you'll notice across the top there are four boxes. I would submit to you there are four main functions in a financial services practice – whether it's a huge practice or a small one. First is the function of marketing. Second is sales. Third is new business and service. Fourth is office management.

I hope that, as a successful producer, you're not involved in anything that has to do with office management. I think if you're reading this book, odds are you're far beyond that but if, by some chance, you picked up this book and you still are doing those things – stop. No, actually STOP! You should be focused on marketing and sales.

Organizational Chart - Single Producer

MARKETING

- $50K – 70K
- Event Management
- Appointment Setting
- Graphics/Brochures, etc.

SALES
(ADVISOR)

- $10-25 Million of Annuity Premium
- $700K – 1.7 Million in Revenue

OFFICE MANAGEMENT

- $40-70K per employee

NEW BUSINESS & SERVICE

- $40-70K per employee

30%–50% MARGINS

So let's say you're a single producer and you're going to see each of your appointments. I would tell you to get a marketing specialist. You might need to pay them $50,000 to $70,000 a year if you want someone who's truly skilled, and what they're going to do is coordinate your event management, appointment setting, brochures, website, radio show – anything that positions your firm to the public. Get that person in place. In my market and region, that could cost $50,000 to $70,000 a year – it may cost slightly more or less in your marketplace. It doesn't matter. You want to hire quality (don't be cheap) and have a high-caliber individual on your team who coordinates your prospecting, spearheads your referral generation, treats your existing clients like royalty and continually communicates your message.

Then we move to sales. Obviously, if you're running a single producer office, "sales" falls on your shoulders, but my hope for you would be that you could continually grow your business to a point at which you hit full sales capacity as an individual. What's that magic number? It obviously varies by producer, but I think as a sole producer in your firm, you should easily be able to do $10 to $25 million in annuity premium. Let's split the difference and say you did $17 million in annuity premium. At a 7 percent commission, $17 million is $1.2 million in revenues. That is a pretty nice gross. Then, you figure out what you're paying for office space and overhead. Let's say 50 percent is going to overhead, leaving you 50 percent of $1.2 million or $600,000 a year. That's a great living that I feel can be done if you are focused, but in order to achieve it in a single producer practice, I'd suggest you *only* be focused on sales. At this level, you are a superstar in your business and, more importantly, you have predictable cash flow because of the way your practice is structured.

With regard to new business and service, again $40,000 to $70,000 is what you could safely budget to get a great employee in your firm for superior new business processing and client service.

In the area of office management – the ordering of supplies, making sure you have business cards and pens on hand, getting the coffee made in the mornings, computers, supplies and things like paying rent and bills and everything else that falls under that umbrella: The key is this position deals with the "backstage" stuff so your other employees can "touch" the clients and prospects.

You can see by this chart that a sole producer with just three employees can have a very, very productive practice. Again, if you're running at a 40 or 50 percent margin on $1.2 million of revenues, you're likely one happy camper. This is an example of rainmaking in which yes, you still have to see all prospects, but you're still embracing a fundamental rainmaking philosophy.

Now, let's look at the next chart that reflects a multiple producer office. This is an office that's doing $3 to $6 million in revenues, and I would submit to you that if you're going to get up to $3 to $6 million, the way to do it is having at least one to two more producers. So, here we are. We've got a marketing department that may now have two employees because you've got to fill the calendar for multiple producers.

Organizational Chart - Multiple Producer Office

MARKETING (2 employees)	SALES (6 employees)	NEW BUSINESS & SERVICE (3 employees)	OFFICE MANAGEMENT (1 employee)	FINANCE (1 employee)
• Seminars	• Joel	• Securities – New Biz	• I.T.	
• Event Management	• Eric	• RIA – New Biz	• Supplies	
• Radio/TV	• Doug	• Annuity & Life	• Greeting	
• Reporting	• Heath	• Product Commission	• Some Assistant Work	
• Special Events	• Christine (Relationship Manager)	• Input		
• Assistant	• Assistant			

You've got a sales department. In my firm, that's comprised of myself, Eric, Doug and Heath. We are all financial advisors. We all see people, though I don't see nearly as many prospects as my associates. We also have Christine, who does nothing but coordinate the calendar – booking appointments, rescheduling appointments, calling people for follow-ups and getting them back in if they haven't been into our office in the last six months. Then, Christine has an assistant who helps with some follow-ups as needed so Christine's primary focus can be filling producers' calendars. You will notice that Christine and her assistant are in the sales department. My former partner and operations manager structured their jobs as administrative, but when my new leadership team truly recognized them as part of the sales team and treated them as such, revenues exploded and they are much happier!

In our firm, we have three employees in new business and service. They take care of all the things you see listed under the new business and service box. We do have an outside firm that does the billing and trading for our managed accounts. Then we have office management, which currently consists of one employee. I also have a finance department, which consists of a CPA who comes in for 15 to 20 hours a week (billing us an independent contractor). She handles paying bills, our payroll and human resources. She also takes care of reconciling the commissions for the other producers and so on.

As you can see here, if you look from left to right in the boxes, I've got two employees in marketing, six employees in sales, three employees in new business and service and one employee in office management.

That's 12 employees plus a financial person. With that team, I am poised to grow to $5 million in revenues, and the profit margins on that $5 million will be very, very healthy. Better yet, under this system, I personally only need to run roughly 10 appointments a week. Thus, 10-12 hours a week, I'm actually meeting with clients. In the time that's left, I have the freedom to create, to market, to come up with new strategies or work on personal growth.

Again, this doesn't have to be your specific model, but I wanted to give you something concrete here under this strategy to draw out what your practice could look like. Use mine as a template if you wish. This is how we're organized, and it works very well.

OBSTACLE 5 — "I'M BOGGED DOWN AND FRUSTRATED WITH NON-REVENUE GENERATING ACTIVITIES."
STRATEGY — MAKE A LIST. / CLEAR THE LIST!

Obstacle number five is this: *"I don't have enough time for revenue generating activities because I'm bogged down by non-revenue generating activities."* Here's the strategy to overcome that obstacle. Literally clear your task list, and refuse to take on any non-revenue generating activities. You pick your top three. <u>STOP</u> doing the rest. Your team should either pick up those activities or you will realize they're not that important. I know what my revenue generating activities are, and they're very simple. They're comprised of three things:

- I communicate to prospective clients and bring them in the door.

- I set the vision and the direction for my company, communicate it to my team and lead and motivate them.
- I generate new sales in selective one-on-one meetings.

Yes, I also do sales. But again, that is communicating – I want you to focus on that for a minute. It could be radio. It could be TV. It could be in a group setting, like a seminar or a church where you have the opportunity to speak. It could be one-on-one or it could be to a group of clients, and they're bringing their friends to an event. But in any sense, you need to communicate your value. Clear your task list, try to get rid of all the things you're not good at. If you're great at appointments, try to just do appointments. If you are good at creative and strategy, try to just do marketing. Now, I know I'm preaching to the choir a little bit here, but the bottom line is some of you know this and you're not doing it.

Stop being frustrated; clear your task list. Personally, frustration for me comes from knowing my potential, having no doubt I can reach it but allowing other things or people to block my arrival to Victory Lane.

OBSTACLE 6 – "I DON'T HAVE THE RIGHT PRODUCERS ON MY TEAM."
STRATEGY – BUILD PROPER SUPPORT STAFF FIRST. THEN FOCUS YOUR TIME ON YOUR TOP THREE ACTIVITIES.

Obstacle number six: You don't have the right producers on the team. You're sitting there saying, "Joel, this all sounds terrific, but I don't know. I don't have the right producers." Okay. Well, start with building the right support staff. Use the single producer model chart I showed you and build the support staff. Bringing a producer in too early is not good if you don't have the support staff in place.

Start with the structure where you're able to run your firm with support and you only do a few things that you're really good at. Then bring in somebody under your wing. You might be able to hire this person on full commission, or you might have to give them a base salary plus commission.

You might give them a little bit of a percentage of everything you write, so maybe they get 5 or 10 percent of everything you write, but they're doing all your paperwork. They're learning the business. They're sitting with you in every single appointment. That's how I train my people. Once I am comfortable with them, which may take 3 – 6 months, then they start trying to add business with existing clients, which helps build up their confidence.

OBSTACLE 7 – "DISTRACTIONS TAKE UP ALL MY ENERGY." STRATEGY – USE THE ENERGY LITMUS TEST. / PROTECT YOUR CONFIDENCE AND ENERGY.

Obstacle number seven: There's too many distractions. I've got questions. I've got service. I've got compliance. Well, I dealt with this much earlier in the book. That story I told you about walking into the office, being excited that I had appointments lined up for opening and closing appointments and getting sucked into all that administrative stuff.

Protect your confidence and energy. Your main job and the main job of your staff is to protect the confidence of the Rainmaker. Do not get distracted by stuff that sucks you down. Here I am writing this book right now, and I'm very, very confident in what I'm saying. I'm focused on what I'm saying. I have a lot of energy as I write this. I'm not distracted by outside things. Protect your confidence and your energy.

Get rid of energy draining distractions. Get rid of anything that sucks your energy. Use the following as a litmus test. Over the next day, two days, three days when you're in your office, keep track of the things that bog you down, where immediately you find out about something and it sucks the energy out of you or you find out about something and it gets you excited. The things that get you excited, that's what you should be doing. There are plenty of people in the world who would love to deal with those things that bog you down. You can't understand how someone would want to deal with those things. You're a unique person with unique abilities and you think everybody's like you. They're not like you. Boy, was this tough for me to learn. People don't think like me.

Not everybody gets excited about the idea of going and buying a business, buying another financial services practice. That's exciting to me. It's a challenge. But somebody else sees, "Oh, my gosh! That's risk. Why can't we just, you know, stay in our cubicle and process the customer service calls?" And they love processing the customer service calls. So, you've got to figure out what gives you energy and get rid of the stuff that doesn't. It sounds simple and it really is. You'd be surprised – if you stop doing stuff, other people will pick it up and get it done or it wasn't that important in the first place.

OBSTACLE 8 — "I LACK CLARITY IN MY SALES PROCESS."
STRATEGY — MAP OUT AND SYSTEMATIZE YOUR PROCESS.

Systematize your process for bringing potential clients into your office and through your funnel. You bring somebody along a continuum: start with a prospect, become a new client, and then servicing them and, if you're doing a good job, they give you introductions and you also write additional business to them.

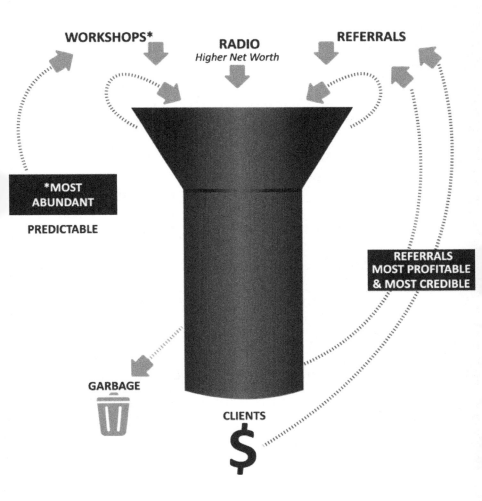

The first part of systematizing the process is to define who your ideal prospect is. Then write out your whole new client process in the form of boxes. What does your new client process look like when they walk into the office or even before that, when they set their appointment? Systematize that process. Write it out. I like to use a big white board and draw boxes, and somebody goes from one box to the next. In our situation, I'll give you an example. They get a direct mail invitation to come to a seminar. That's box number one. Box number two is they call us to make a reservation for the seminar. What does that process look like? Box number three: They've made a reservation to the seminar and they get a call the day before confirming that they're going to be there.

WHO DO YOU WANT TO ATTRACT?

- Fiscally conservative
- Value advice and expertise
- "Self-made" individuals
- $500,000-$2,000,000 in investable assets (our sweet spot)
- We're working with more people with $2-$3M in investable assets
- Understand who you are competing against in your sweet spot

Now, in these boxes there are other little things that are going on, but I just want you to focus on the big picture right now. They get a confirmation call. The next box would be they show up at the seminar and I present, or I might have one of my advisors present. (I do most of the seminars; again, I'm the communicator for the team, and I communicate our philosophy.) We have some fun. The goal of the seminar is to get somebody to book an appointment.

So the next box is they schedule an appointment.

The next box is they get a letter in the mail saying, "Thank you for coming in. We're excited to see you. Here are some things that you should bring that will be helpful for you," and "Here's your appointment." And then they get a confirmation the day before the appointment, just to make sure that they're on. If an appointment's going to fall off, I want to know it a day before. I don't want any no shows. I would rather have them cancel. I'd rather know I've got an extra hour to go to the gym or to have lunch or return some calls. Maybe I'll call one of those clients who I feel I've outgrown, and now I can reach back and do a little half-hour review with them. That will make us both feel good.

The next box is going to be they come in for that appointment. What does that look like? What kind of forms do I use to do a fact finder, a discovery meeting?

The next box is going to be I schedule a second appointment or we let them go. And then they come in for that second appointment. Maybe they become a client, but between that first and second appointment, obviously, there's some case preparation that goes on, so that's a separate box on its own.

If they become a client, well, that's a process, right? We do some paperwork. My back office processes the paperwork and then once their money moves over here, we always have what we call a delivery appointment. It might not be to deliver an annuity contract, because maybe they're just a securities or a managed money client, but we kind of have this delivery appointment where, now that their money has moved, their anxiety is, "Did I make the right decision?" So I've got a box for that delivery appointment, which relieves their anxiety.

Then we've got a box for how do we get referrals, how do we get introductions to that person's friends. And then, again, the review process. So these are all different boxes that let you systematize your process. Make it simple. Don't make it too complicated – I think if you have more than 15 boxes, you're making this too complicated. Try to consolidate, but systematize the process. And then, guess what you do next – you decide what part of that you do not need to be involved in. You make more money saying no than you make saying yes, and that's saying no to the things you don't want to be involved in. I'll bet when you figure out where you really make your money, you make all your money in a given week, you make all your money in about a three- to five-hour time span and the rest of it is just crap. Get rid of all this other stuff and now, instead of working three to five hours a week, you work six to 10 hours a week in your unique ability and you double your revenues.

I bet you're only spending about 20 percent of your time making money. What if you get rid of the other 80 percent of the stuff that you're not making money on and just double the 20 percent? Wow! That'd be exciting, wouldn't it?

OBSTACLE 9 – "MY TEAM WON'T GO ALONG."
STRATEGY – GET THEM INVOLVED EARLY, COMMUNICATE YOUR VISION AND EXPLAIN HOW THEY WILL BENEFIT.

Get total buy-in from your team. You've got to communicate this stuff to your team. They will gravitate toward the status quo and what they've seen. Remember, no matter how uncomfortable someone is, psychology tells us that they'd rather deal with what they know than what they don't know. This is why, if you've ever studied family origin issues, if somebody comes from a chaotic family growing up they feel more comfortable being in chaos than creating a life that is not chaotic. To get emotionally healthy, the person has to break out of the comfort zone, but it is hard. Your staff will gravitate toward the status quo. You've got to get buy-in from your team. Protect them from events they have outgrown. Get them to stretch. Build an entrepreneurial culture.

Here's something else to watch out for. As I grow in this business, I've made the mistake from time to time of getting excited about some training I heard about and sending a staff person to the training and then they come back and go, "Joel, it looked like it was going to be training, but when I got out there it was just a recruiting event for the FMO." Well, it would have been nice for me to know that ahead of time.

Another one would be, "Joel, I went out there and we're so far above everybody else in that room, including the instructors, as a business that I really didn't get much out of it," or "I only got one or two ideas out of it." Protect yourself and your people from training that's not helpful.

Now, I believe in training. We spend well into the six figures on training every year for myself and my people; just make sure you're not sending them to training that looks really great but is way too basic.

OBSTACLE 10 – "I CAN'T POSSIBLY MANAGE ALL OF THIS. I CAN'T CONTROL IT."

STRATEGY – BUILD WORKING LEADERS BUT NOT LAYERS OF MANAGEMENT.

About a year and a half ago, in April 2012, I had just bought out a former partner of mine and that former partner was the operations manager of the firm. She had structured a firm where there was me and then there was this middle layer of management, which was her, and then there was everybody else. And we had this system where people didn't know what other people were doing. There was a lot of frustration in the company. We were almost structured like a corporation or the military where we'd have this chain of command, and I didn't realize it was causing so many problems until I had an outside consultant who I respect greatly come in. He confidentially interviewed all of the employees and found out a few of them were about to quit. At the time, I had bought out this person and she was still on as an employee. I thought that in order for the company to not "fall apart," we needed this full year of transition.

We made a couple decisions that were very tough. One was that we did not need the operations manager, former partner in place anymore. We decided that our people were ready to lead themselves, and we created teams and in each team there was a working leader. Now, it's very important that you understand this. In my team, for instance, if you go back to my organizational chart, you have my new business and service team and that consists of three employees. There is a working team leader amongst that team, so they're all on the same level. The team leader is accountable to me for getting the job done, so the only time that team leader is, in a sense, in the hot seat is if he's not getting the job done as it's been communicated to him. Everybody jumps in to work together. We're too small to have this attitude that one person's job is this and my job is to do this and we don't cross.

We don't want any layers of management. Build your team leaders.

Now, I don't know, but I think you can get up to about 20 employees before you have to create any layers of management, and I'll be there pretty soon. I'll bet this consultant that I worked with – his name is Mike Meek, a tremendous individual – I bet he has ideas where you can get even bigger than 20 employees without creating layers of management. Layers just create problems and what I found was there were all kinds of things going on in the company that I didn't know about. Resentment was building up in the company. So build team leaders, not layers of management.

You'll also notice on my organization chart that I'm right in there. I'm in the mix. I do some marketing. I do a little bit of sales. I'm the Rainmaker. I create traffic. But there's a peer group here and I believe they really appreciate each other. As a boss, I might not know everything that goes on, but we've got a great system in place.

OBSTACLE 11 – "WILL INCREMENTAL GROWTH BE WORTH IT?"
STRATEGY - SET HUGE GOALS TO TRANSFORM YOUR BUSINESS.

And here, this one is fun – a little bit of a shift: <u>Set huge goals</u>. Here's a great exercise, again, another thing that I've learned at strategic coaching. Take your business, take one factor in your business, such as profits, revenues, employees. If you're running a charity, it would be the amount of money you give away. Multiply it by 10. Set a massive goal. Say, "If I was ten times bigger than I am today. . ." Now it doesn't have to be total revenues. It could be something else, but let's just say for me it was total revenues. I grew my business from $4.1 million that we did last year to $41 million. What would that company have to look like for me to do that? Would I have to do different things? Absolutely, I'd have to do different things.

If that's too big for you to get your arms around, just double your business, okay? If I did $4.1 million, what would my company look like if I did $8.2 million of total revenues? I'm not talking about premium. I'm talking about dollars that come into the company, fees or commission. Would I have to do things differently? Absolutely. Would my staff have to do things differently? Certainly. Would we have different structures in place? Definitely. Would I need more employees? Probably. Would we have to stop talking with certain people, like certain prospects? Maybe. Would we have to decide that there are certain lines of business we won't want to be involved in because the cost of our energy is too high, or maybe the cost of doing it is too high or there's just not enough time in the day?

Now that's an exciting way to approach your business. So think of your business right now. Forget about the 10 times for a minute. Just take two times. Say you did $1 million of revenues last year into you as a company. You did $1 million of commission. Turn around and write out what your company would have to look like to do $2 million of commission. I bet you you're going to find out that – guess what? You don't write checks anymore. You don't worry about payroll anymore. You don't worry about compliance any more. You get other people to do that stuff. You focus on those few things that you're good at. Once again, for me it's setting strategic direction for the company, communicating a marketing message to the public, and making sure we're delivering on our promises.

Business Philosophy

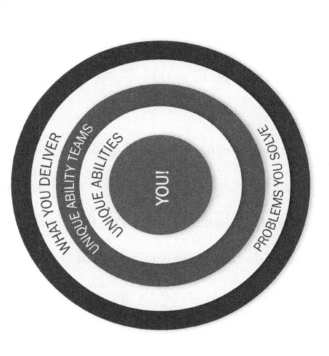

Look at the diagram, "Business Philosophy," and in the middle it says, "You." Then it says, "Unique Abilities." The next ring out is, "Unique Ability Team." The next ring out is what you deliver and the problems you solve. It starts with you. What are your unique strengths? Your unique abilities? You've got to hone in. The bigger you get, the more you've got to work in the center of this.

As a small business, you can afford to do everything. When I started out in the business selling life insurance policies, I focused on the need to do the sales, to do the marketing, to go out and deliver. I had to tell everybody about all the problems I solved and so on and so forth. But as I grew, I get more and more toward the center of that ring and was able to focus on what I'm really good at. I got a team around me to help me deliver that, ultimately, to the public.

Remember, you get paid to start things, not necessarily finish them. There are other people who are better at finishing things than you are.

OBSTACLE 12 - "I CAN'T AFFORD THIS." OR "I NEED TO PERSONALLY KEEP MY SALES UP FOR THE CASH FLOW." STRATEGY - MAKE DECISIONS AND DREAM AS IF MONEY IS NO LONGER AN ISSUE.

When making big decisions, what if money wasn't an issue? What would you do? This is a big one. What if you never, ever for the rest of your life had to make a decision based on whether you could afford it or because you would make more money? What if you just made a decision because it was the right thing or because you thought it might be fun to try it? Wouldn't that be awesome? I'm getting excited thinking about it. Maybe you want to take out a journal and write down what would you do if money didn't matter. What would your business look like if you never had to worry about making enough to pay your employees, to pay your rent? How would your family dynamics change if you never had to worry about paying the bills, or if you weren't focused on buying that vacation house or that nicer car?

If you had all the stuff you wanted, what kind of decisions would you make in your life? That's a powerful way to approach important decisions because then, when you start making decisions based on other factors, the future is unlimited.

About 11 or 12 years ago, I joined a program The Strategic Coach and we did a very, very interesting exercise. We kind of mapped out our lives with Mr. Sullivan, although it wasn't him at the time; I wasn't making enough money to get him as a coach, so I worked with one of his junior coaches. By the way, Sullivan started coaching one-on-one and then he added junior coaches, just like I started one on one and now I have associate advisors. But one of his junior coaches said, "We're going to do a little exercise called the Lifetime Extender. You pick the day you're going to die. You pick the age at which you're going to die. It sounds kind of weird, but here we go." I think I picked, at the time, 77. I think my grandfather had died at 77, so I thought at 77, I would die.

He said, "Okay. Extend your life by five years." Move from 77 to 82.

Pretend for those five years, ages 77 to 82, you had no health problems. You had all the money you ever needed. You never had to worry about finances or health at all. What would you do with your life? What would your day-to-day activities be? And he had us write and then he said, "You know what you should be doing right now? Living your life with that list you just made." Well, this kind of goes back to the question, what decisions would you make if money was not an issue. What would you do with your life? I think that's a great strategy.

CONCLUSION

I've laid out 12 strategies for you. I want to take you back to the very beginning of this book, when I talked about some of the frustrations you may be feeling right now. You want to grow, you just don't know how. You feel stifled. You come to these conferences. You get all motivated, you get back to your office and the energy gets yanked right out from under you. You write all these great plans, and you can't seem to follow through on them because you get distracted. The Rainmaker Solution is my answer to the question of *how do I transform from being out of control and limited to being relaxed and confident.*

You can have more predictable cash flow. You can have more personal time. Creative flexibility will be abundant. You'll be able to operate on the right side of your brain instead of the left side reacting to "stuff." You'll be able to be <u>present</u> in every situation. It's tough, especially in the world we live in, but you can be present if you're at your kid's sporting event or your kid's dance recital. If you're with your spouse or significant other on a date, you can be present. If you're in the office in a staff meeting, you're actually present. When somebody is talking about something, talking from the heart, and it's not important to you and your mind is off somewhere else, you're not present. You can actually be present and caring about your employees, and you can be people focused, not problem focused.

These strategies I've laid in the book hopefully will give you an insight into what I have done in my business. We've increased more than 10-fold since I began working as an entrepreneur and actually, we're up about 15 times. I'm looking forward to growing another 10 times. I don't know how I'll get there, but I didn't know how I was going to get there 10 years ago either. These strategies can help you.

They can help you build a business and create fulfillment in your life. You'll be satisfied, relaxed, and your business will not be totally dependent upon you. You will truly embrace the entrepreneurial lifestyle.

For more information on how the Rainmaker Solution can change your business, go to the Game Changer app on iAdvisor located on www.advisorsexcel.com. You'll find resources available to you as an exclusive member of the group that purchased or received this book as a tool to improve your personal and business life.

Made in the USA
Middletown, DE
10 September 2025

17379751R00071